Dedication

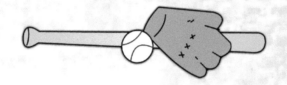

To my boys Conner and Nolan, you are my inspiration
and my loves. May you always have stinky socks
from playing hard and dreaming big!

To my husband Patrick for believing in me
and supporting all of my crazy dreams.
I love you with all of my heart.

The Legend of the
Stinky Sock

Laura Riley

Illustrated by Chris E Hammond

Copyright © 2021 by Laura Riley

ISBN 978-1-7368975-0-8

The Legend
of the
Stinky Sock

Laura Riley

My name is Conner, and my Little League baseball team, the Rockets, were off to a terrible start to our season.

We had lost four games in a row without scoring one run.

Tiger Field

SPITFIRES	1	0	5	2	1	9
ROCKETS	0	0	0	0	0	0

RILEY FIELD

ROCKETS	0	0	0	0	0	0
HOT DOGS	0	0	2	6	2	10

HOME RUN PARK

ROCKETS	0	0	0	0	0	0
SPITFIRES	3	6	1	1	1	12

EMMET PARK

GUMBALLS	4	3	2	1	3	13
ROCKETS	0	0	0	0	0	0

We needed something to get us out of this awful losing streak—and that something was the Stinky Sock.

I know it sounds crazy, but after we lost our last game my Dad told me about "The Legend of the Stinky Sock".

According to the myth, there is a stinky, dirty sock that gives you magical baseball powers to hit home runs, throw strikes, and make incredible plays.

My dad said that you need to complete three tasks to make the Stinky Sock appear.

The first task is to hit a home run. I had never hit one before, but I was determined. I grabbed my little brother Nolan, and we headed to the field.

I stood at home plate, eyes focused on the ball, bat in the air—then came the pitch. I swung and missed! It was horrible.

When I swung the bat, I spun in a circle and landed on my bottom.

When I got up, I realized a big wad of gum was stuck to my pants. Nolan was laughing hysterically as I pulled off the gooey mess.

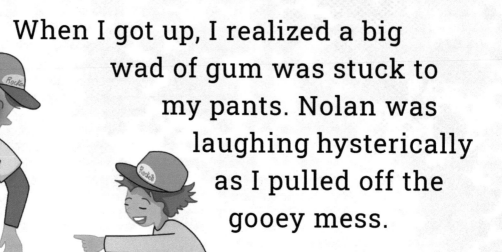

Even more determined, I told Nolan to pitch to me again. It took sixty pitches for me to finally hit one magical home run!

The legend said that you needed to field fifty ground balls and catch fifty pop flies.

Nolan hit the balls, and I fielded them.

We got off to a rocky start. With the crack of the bat, Nolan hit a fly ball right to me.

However, instead of catching the ball, it smacked me right in the face.

My efforts to catch the next one were just as bad. When I went to grab the ball,

I tripped over second base and landed right in a big puddle of mud. When I got up, there was mud in my eyes and mud dripping off my chin.

I wanted to go home, but I needed to get that Stinky Sock. I did not catch the next forty-six balls Nolan hit to me.

By number forty-seven, my luck had changed. I caught every ball after that!

Finally, I was on to the last task. This one seemed easy. I just needed to play catch for a half hour.

Nolan and I tossed the ball around until our arms ached from playing so long.

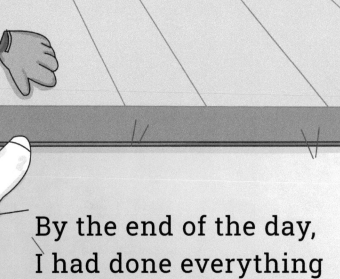

By the end of the day,
I had done everything
the legend required.

I was tired, smelly, and covered in dust and mud.

I wondered when the sock would appear, so I asked my dad.

He smiled and said, "Just look down at your feet."

Confused, I looked down at my filthy socks.

"YOUR socks are the Stinky Socks," he said.

"What?" I replied.

What?

"The only magic in life is the magic you create," my dad explained. "You have to practice and work hard to get better."

I was mad. I went to bed disappointed.

The next day, we had a game. Just in case my dad was wrong about the socks' magic, I put on my pair from the day before.

They were stinky
and very dirty.

stinky!

TEXAS

Soon it was my turn to bat and, wouldn't
you know it? I hit a colossal home run.

I even caught a fly ball and threw
a runner out at first.

The Rockets won our first game of the season.

RILEY FIELD

| ROCKETS | 0 | 0 | 1 | 2 | 1 | 4 |
| HOT DOGS | 1 | 1 | 0 | 1 | 0 | 3 |

I guess maybe my dad was on to something. Gosh, I hate it when my dad is right!

About the Author

LAURA RILEY is a children's book author and stay-at-home mother. Having two rambunctious young boys of her own she knows how to capture the attention of budding minds with humor and topics that will inspire them to read.

Her passion for telling a compelling story began in college where she studied journalism. Laura's love for writing continued when she went on to work for the local NBC station KOAA in Colorado Springs and Fox 59 in Indianapolis.

Laura grew up in the Chicago suburbs and currently lives in the Dallas area with her husband Patrick and children Conner and Nolan. She was motivated to write her first book as the result of teaching her first grader how to compose his own story for a school project. His excitement and creativity encouraged her to complete a life long dream to write her own book.

About the Illustrator

CHRIS E HAMMOND is a children's picture book designer and illustrator with a studio in Myrtle Creek, Oregon. Here's what he says about his work: "My work with kid's books brings me back to my own childhood and many good times I had growing up in rural Oregon. Often, the process of drawing the settings and landscapes helps me reconnect with nature which I really enjoy.

CPSIA information can be obtained
at www.ICGtesting.com
Printed in the USA
BVHW061133170821
614613BV00010B/649